First of All

A Big thanks To you For

Supporting me . . .

How To Earn Money From Youtube

BY **SRI GADIRAJU** ...

I Dedicate this book to my Dad who has been taking care of me from the day I have born , who is there with me all the time , in my ups and Downs . Thank you Dad for being a good friend .

Yours lovingly ,

G.Srivathsav

Preface :

Few Years Back , I have started a youtube channel of my own with a Branding after my own name " **SRI GADIRAJU** " .

After I have faced Lots of Ups and Downs in this online industry . I decided that no one should face these kinds of hurdles never again and I thought every one should know how to generate passive Income , that I have described in this book . I have clearly explained how to over come the difficulties that you face as a beginner and intermediate , being a youtuber .

Please excuse me if there are any typo's and Errors in the sentences because I have typed all the content on my own and that too with in a day . . .

> **Turn the Page and start Earning . . . By** Learning . . .

Contents ...

21)   Can A Person Choose Youtube as a full time Job ?

22)   Is it ok to copy content from another youtube channel ?

23)   What is Content Violation ?

24)   What should we do When our videos get Blocked ?

25)   Can We Have Two Youtube Channels ?

26)   How does collaboration with other channel works . Is

collaboration really Needed ?

27)   Making use of the QR codes

28)   Youtube Simplified **– A quick Review**

<u># 1 * CREATING YOUTUBE CHANNEL</u>

Sign in to youtube on your mobile Device or in a browser in your computer . For signing in to youtube you don't have to create any account you can directly login by using your google account ID , in the sense Gmail ID and Password .

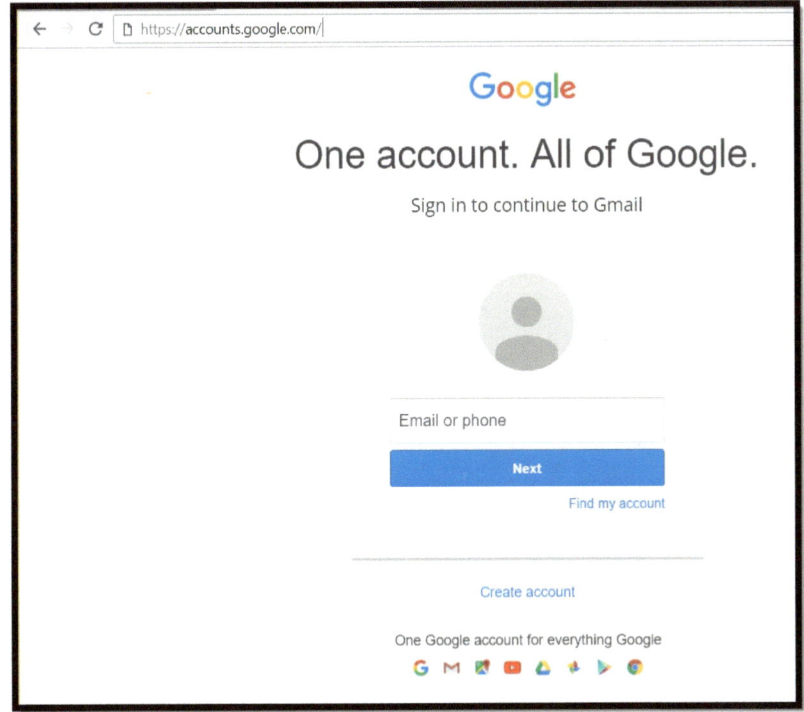

1) Go to your **channel list**
2) There will be an option to " **Create a new channel** " and one more option is to " **Use an existing channel account** " .
3) Fill Out the details to name your new youtube channel and **verify your account** .

You have get verified to upload videos . . .

To " **GET PARTNER VERIFIED** "

You need to give your mobile number and after that an OTP will
be sent to your mobile phone –
Once you verify that you will get " partner verified " text beside
your account picture . . .
Like this . . .

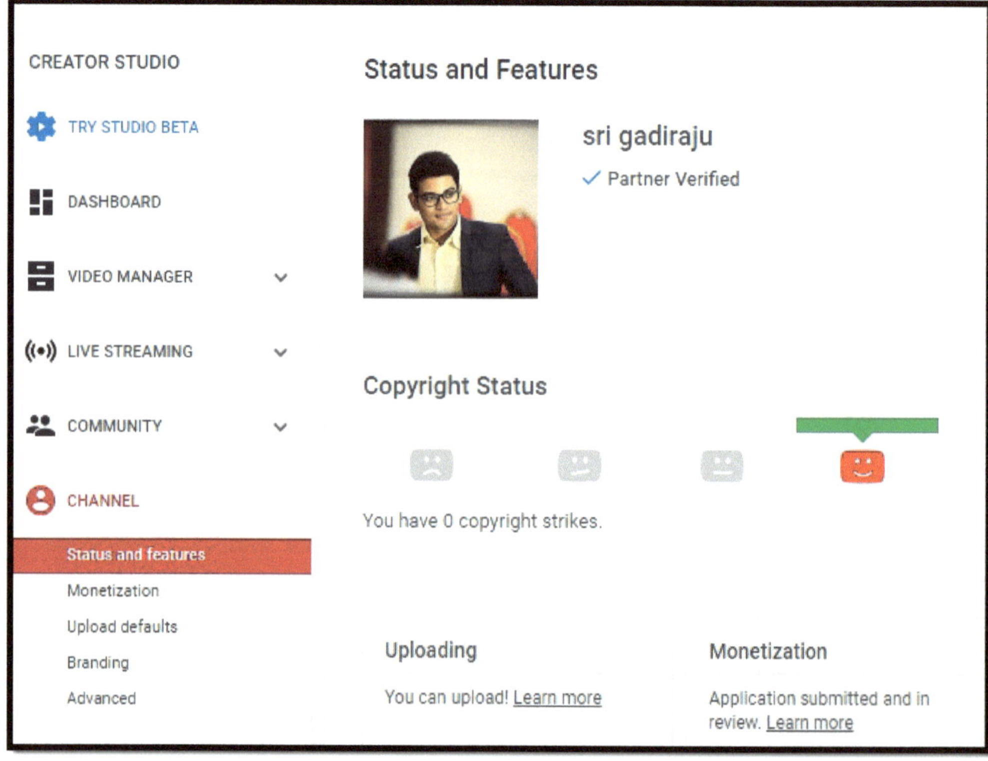

The Verification process involves lot of steps that you will get to
know once you perform the above steps .

While Creating youtube channel take advice from any social media influencer related to your content if you know any in person .

so that they can help you not only in guiding you but also in sharing your content on their pages there by increasing the traffic to your channel .

You can go to the account settings by clicking on **" Creator Studio "**

Option .

Below that option you will two options .

 One is to **Add account** and another one is to **Sign out .**

If you want to add another youtube account by using another gmail then you can do that by clicking on Add account option .

That will ask you to sign in with another google account which in turn creates another youtube channel .

So If anyone wants two youtube channels with two google accounts that they have , they can follow this way .

You can see a screenshot of the creator studio option in the next page .

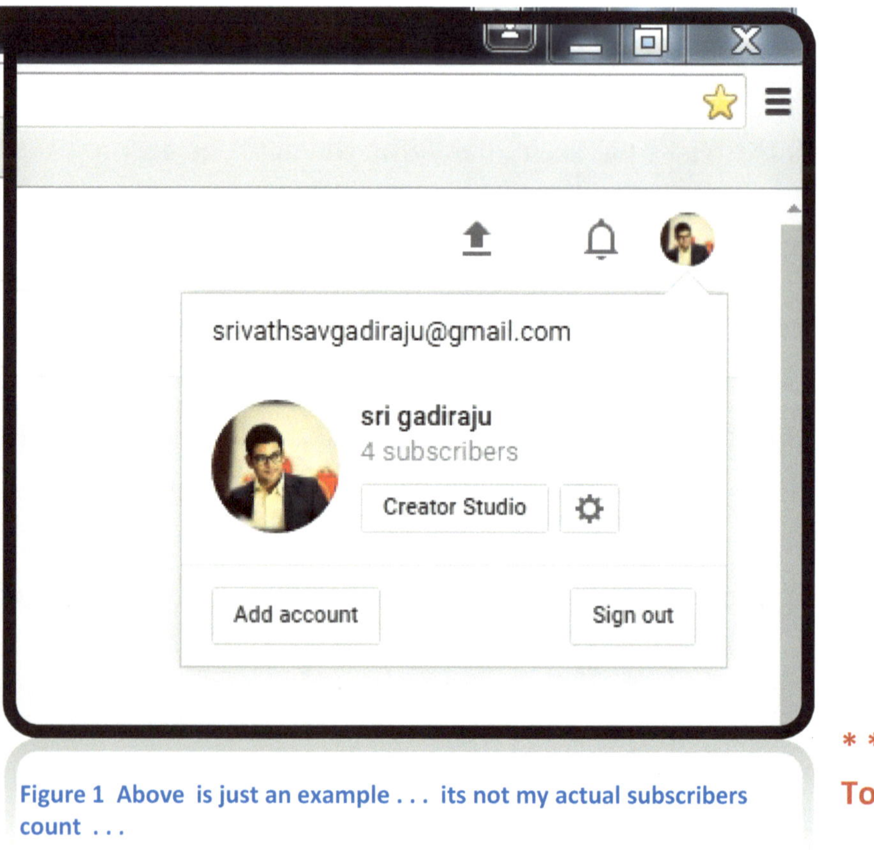

Perform any operations on your channel or to perform any modifications to your videos and settings and stuff like that the first thing you need to get used to is . . . Creator studio * * * To

As mentioned before You can go to your youtube account settings by clicking on **" Creator Studio " Option** .

<u>**2 * CHOOSE THE PEOPLE THAT YOU WANT TO FOCUS ON**</u> …

First of all you have to be sure about the content that you want to post on youtube .

Lets just say it is about Fitness then you have to start targeting people that have passion for fitness by uploading videos about fitness and stuff . If you have a passion for cooking then upload content about cooking .

If you have a passion for painting then upload videos about painting . If you know how to play a guitar then record videos of you playing guitar .

If you have a Knowledge about certain topics then upload content about the topics that you are good at . It all depends on your interest .

But , You have to be sure about the type of videos that you upload otherwise you will end up creating all kinds of videos and that leads to a situation where the audience find it awkward to stay tuned to your channel .

Because the first thing audience wants from you is consistency .

So Don't try to target lot of categories . Instead Pick one subject that you are good at and start creating content on it . Automatically that particular group of audience will get attracted to your channel . There is a saying that " similar kind of videos in your channel will be helpful for the channel to grow rather than having different kinds of targets " .

For Example , there is a youtube channel called **" Slo Mo Guys "** , in that youtube channel they upload every kind of Experiments that they do in Slow motion . That's it . . .

They became Famous youtubers . Their speciality is nothing but consistency and keeping it simple , at the same time targeting the audience who loves to watch videos in slow motion . Likewise , you can do what you are good at .

But the content that you upload should be Informative or atleast entertaining .

If there is no Information in the video Atleast there should be Entertainment in the content that you choose .

If you already have a youtube channel and there are some videos on your channel which are of no use …

Just Delete those videos .

I know it's hard to do that , but it is important to step away from your self into shoes of outsider from time to time . In the sense , you should think from the viewer's perspective .

Taking a look at your youtube channel and revaluating what is there will give you an idea about the old stuff that you have uploaded .

Don't make your youtube channel a Mess , otherwise you will end up loosing your audience .

ne such example is my previous youtube channel itself . You can go to my channel using the link :

www.youtube.com/user/srivathsavgadiraju

On that channel , I have got subscribers Near to thousand and my page views have crossed lakhs but that channel is a big mess . Actually it became a big mess , Because I have selected lot of topics to target on . . .

Hence , I ended up uploading irrelavent content because of which lot of users have unsubscribed .

So out of experience I am telling this to you guys . Don't target lot of topics .

If you target more people then your youtube channel will also be a big mess Like mine ...

You can opt for two or may be three topics atmost , that too if you wish you have more content to share .

3 * UPLOADING VIDEOS

After creating your brand channel now its time to upload videos .

If you know how to upload a video you can skip this page . . .

How to upload a video :

To upload videos using your mobile phone you can click on share by choosing the video that you want to upload and then click on the youtube Icon in the share options .

To upload videos using your computer you can click on Up arrow mark

As shown here right before the sign in option .

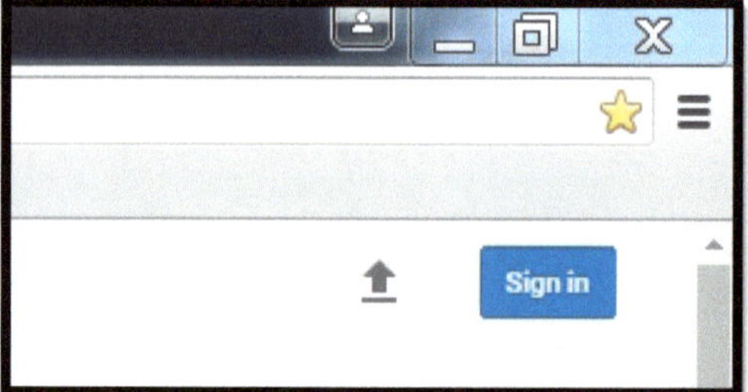

This option will be shown in the right side corner of your web browser .

Once you click on the up arrow mark it will ask you to sign in using your google account (Gmail) . . .

Yes . . . you heard me right you don't need any credentials for your youtube account . you can use your google / gmail account ID and password itself for your youtube .

Once you have signed in to your account then you can see the sign in option changed in to your account Icon . . .

As shown Here . . .

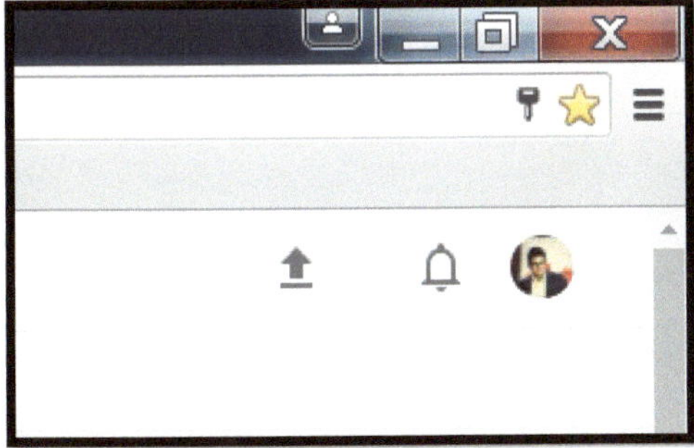

How the Video Should be :

The First thing you have to keep in mind is the **Quality of the video** .

I am not telling you to put 4K videos .

But the videos should be good enough to watch .

Coming to the video Playtime , it does n't have be too long – making it boring and it does n't have to be too short – Making it difficult for monetising .

Because if the video time is too less there will be less chances for the youtube algorithm to place Ads on your videos .

In the next page I have shown you a screenshot of How the creator studio options will look like in a desktop web browser .

If you want to do any operations by making use of mobile phone then you can download the creator studio application from google play store that is available for the android devices .

After you have Uploaded the video you can manage to edit or do further operations by clicking on creator studio .

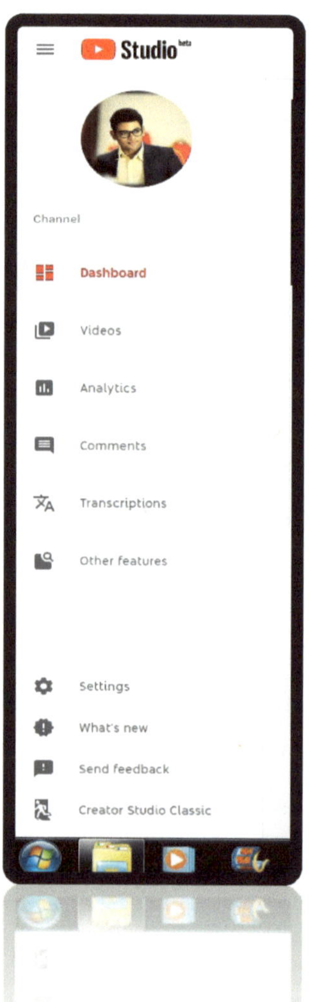

One more thing you should be Focusing on while uploading Videos is to make sure that you don't fall in to the category copyright

In the sense you should not violate any copyrights , If by chance you violate any copy rights again and again it leads to termination of your youtube account or you may lose your monetization option forever – then you will end up creating another channel and you have to start from the scratch all over again . you don't want that right . . . !

So . . .

Never and ever Upload any video that is not yours . If the youtube algorithm finds out that you have taken someone's content and used it to make money then youtube will block that video and will send you a mail to remove that video .

Not only video content , but using any audio that is not yours may also leads to copy right violation . Because Even audio should be your own or else you can use youtube's Free Audio to add in to your videos , if you want . Apart from that you should not upload any content that is not yours .

For example , Uploading a movie is the biggest copy right violation that anyone can do . Never do that . otherwise you may lose your channel permenantly .

Meanwhile the money that is generated by means of that video will be sent to the video's original owner .

4 * CREATING PLAYLISTS

After Creating and uploading videos . Now it is time to categorize them and set those videos in playlists depending up on the type of the videos that you have in your youtube channel .

As you can make videos into private , unlisted and public categories – Likewise , you can make the playlist itself private or public or unlisted depending up on your choice .

Private playlist means No one will be able to see your playlist .

Public playlist means anyone can see your playlist .

Unlisted Playlist means that , who ever has the link to that specific playlist that particular person can be able to see it .

These are the steps that you need to do for uploading a video in to playlist :

➜ Firstly , Start with a video that you want to be placed in the playlist . Choose the videos .

➜ Under the video section click **add to**

➜ You will be having options to Select " watch Later " or a Select a Playlist that you have already created if any . Click on **Select playlist**

➔ If playlist is not created yet , then click on **create new playlist**

for a playlist to be created .

➔ You will be having a Drop Down Menu in the settings , Make Use

of this Drop down box to **select your playlist privacy setting**

➔ Now the final step , Click **" create "**

It is as simple as that .

You can also manage your playlists by going into video manager section . . .

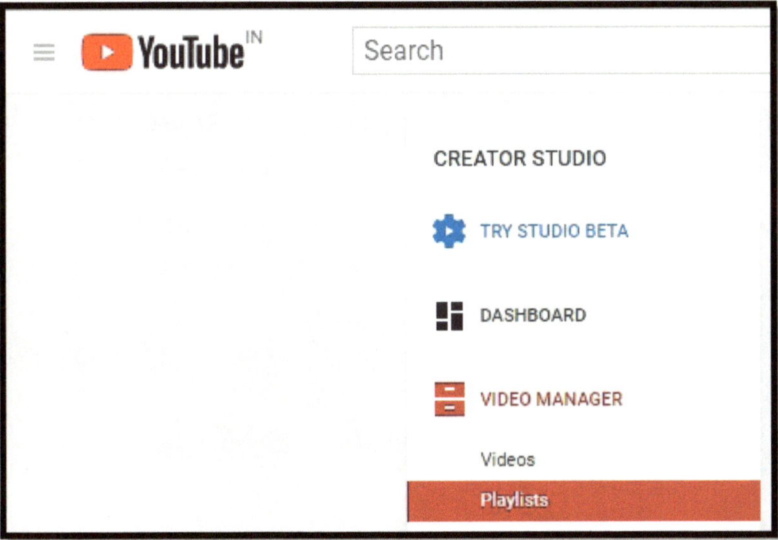

5 * SHARING CONTENT ON SOCIAL MEDIA

For any youtube channel to become famous , the videos in that channel has to get more views . But for that to happen you need to know **SEO** (Search Engine Optimization) that is another case . As of now we have covered the basics so let me explain you how can we get maximum number of views by sharing the video links to your social media pages . Youtube will give you an option to share the video after you have uploaded it . you can copy the video's link by clicking on share button available below the video . share the video to your **facebook page** , **Instagram account** , **whatsapp** and **Twitter** as well as **snapchat** .

By Doing this your friends will get to know that you have started a **" Youtube channel "** and they will support you by sharing the links further to their friends . Also mention in all of your videos in your youtube channel that to connect to you by making use of your social media accounts .

Back in the days I used to put the Logos of all the social media accounts and I used to embed the links on the Logos .

<u>6 * MONITOR YOUR DATA</u>

Lot of people Neglect this . . . !

Monitoring the number of views and likes and dislikes and the money that you are getting for a particular video all these things matter ...

Because that's how you know what kind of stuff is getting popular in your channel and how much revenue is being generated by that . There by you can further manage your content effectively once you analyse the data . There are lot of softwares available online to analyse your youtube data more precisely . One such software is " **Tubebuddy** " .

If you Guys are not familiar with that tool then don't worry I will be explaining about it to you guys in 17th chapter . But for now we will learn how to make use of youtube Analytics to monitor your Data on your youtube channel .

In the next page I have shown an example picture of how the analytics option will be helpful in showing the statics of the amount that we are earning . . .

you can make use of analytics option in creator studio settings to monitor the amount that you are earning and the views that you are getting . . .

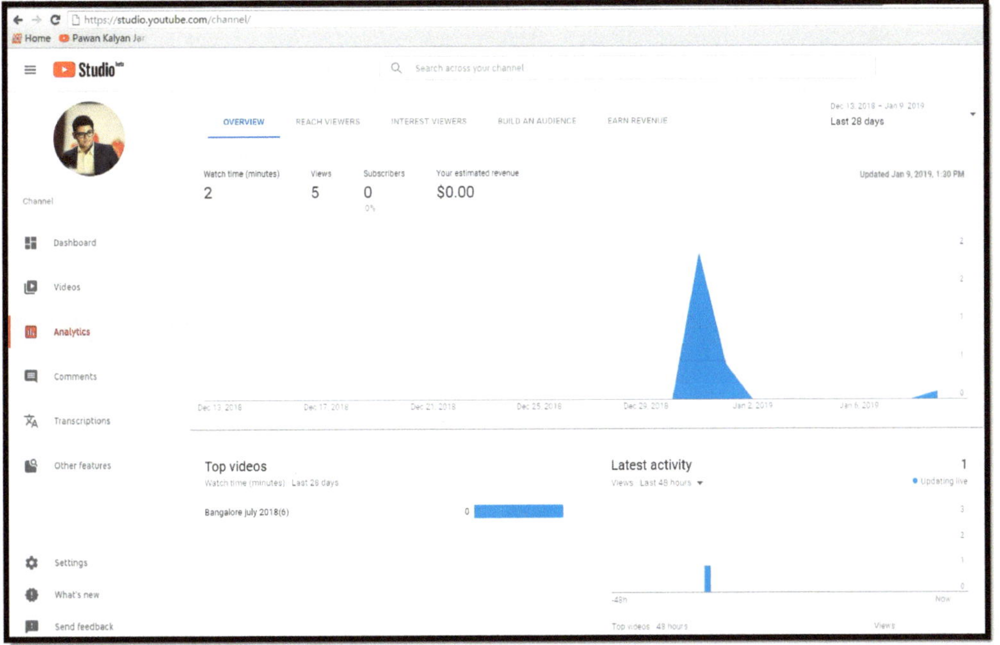

<u>7 * BUILD YOUR COMMUNITY</u>

Another thing a youtuber needs to focus on is building a community . If you rely only on the people that you know then the chances are your channel will not reach more number of people …

Youtube Creator Academy suggests us to follow these 4 steps for Building a Solid Base Foundation to maintain our community :

1) Be Authentic with your audience

2) Share your Creation Story

3) Develop healthy rituals specific for your channel

4) Be a responsible youtuber

HOW CAN BEING AUTHENTIC WITH YOUR AUDIENCE HELPS YOU IN BUILDING COMMUNITY ?

The First thing you have to keep in mind is that it doesn't happen overnight and it is an evolutionary process . Let's discuss about the benefits of building a community by being authentic .

i)   You will have a Deeper connection with your audience which leads to channel growth .

ii)   If Viewers have positive interactions with you , they are more likely to share your videos to their community as well .

It is said that , " when creators take some quality time to interact authentically with their community , it will in turn encourages audience to participate ", and there by your fanbase will be increased

SHARE YOUR CREATION STORY

Sharing your story is an effective strategy for the viewers to relate to you and get attached to you . your " Creation story " is nothing but the journey that you have made till now to achieve the position that you are in right now . you should tell your viewers the thing that led you to youtube .

HOW DEVELOPING RITUALS SPECIFIC FOR YOUR CHANNEL CAN BUILD YOUR COMMUNITY ?

First let me make this clear , Rituals are nothing but repeated activities that you do . For Example , your unique video formats and the locations that you go for to shoot the videos and the slang or lingo that you use in your videos all these things makes viewers attached to you if you make this a consistent habit . Because Viewers will get use to your slang after a period of time . so try to stick to one language or one slang . Uploading videos in regular intervals and being consistent is the ultimate key .

Also Keep in mind one thing that the slang that you use makes a lot of difference for your viewers to feel like they are insiders .

HOW BEING A RESPONSIBLE YOUTUBER CAN HELP YOU BUILD YOUR COMMUNITY

Lot of youtubers have good content published in their youtube channels and also good thumbnails and keywords used for the videos . But the reason people are not getting interested to such channels is probably because those youtubers have not focused on interacting and communicating with the audience .

It is important for a youtuber to see all the comments and to give reply to those comments .

<u>8 * SELECTING THE TYPE OF THE ADS TO BE DISPLAYED</u>

As you know , there are different types of Ads that one will get while watching youtube videos . You will be paid once these ads start showing up on your videos or else you can make use of these ads to promote your channel as well .

These are the different types of Ads :

a) Skippable Video Ads or True View Ads

b) Non – Skippable Ads

c) Overlay Ads

d) Display Ads

e) Sponsored Cards

f) Bumper Ads

You can make use of these ads to earn money by allowing the Ads to be displayed on your video that is nothing but monetization . I will be explaining the topics of monetization later . But for now we will go through the types of Ads available .

If you want to choose the Ads that can be displayed on your videos –

You can go for " **Upload Defaults** " settings and Enable all the Ads

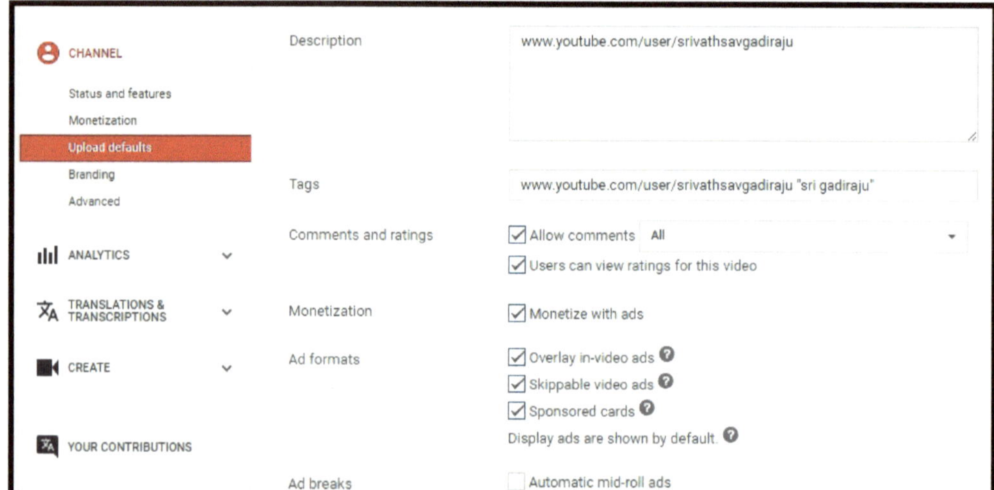

a) True View Ads :

The True View Ads in other terms the **skippable video ads** are the best when it comes to drive brand engagement on youtube . These Ads can be skipped after 5 seconds . Even you know about this right … ?

The Skippable ads comes in two formats . One is **In-Stream Ads** and the other is **Discovery Ads .**

In stream Ads are like this :-

The Ad Location will be on youtube videos , apps , games , videos in google's display pop up screens .

The In stream video length will be maximum of 3 minutes .

Clicks will be going to websites or Blogs .

Discovery Ads are like this :

For these types of Ads the Ad Location will be on youtube videos and as well as on search results that the search engine displays when you search for something and the additional benefit here we have is that there is no limit of video length for these kinds of Ads . These Ads will be displayed as " Related Videos " as well .

The clicks will go to Website or blog or directly to a Video .

b) Non – Skippable Youtube Ads :

Non – Skippable Ads are paid on clicks per Minute Basis . Even though these Ads are too long in duration these Ads are very powerful because you will be getting more income because of the longer duration of the Ads .

Its true that most viewers wish those non – skippable ads were not there at all .

Youtube algorithm knows this ...

That is the reason why the previous year the youtube officially removed the 30 second un skippable ad format .

Now the time limit for Non – Skippable Ads is 15 to 20 Seconds .

c) Overlay Ads :

Youtube has a special option for you guys to display ads at bottom of your video . In these overlay ads again there are two different types of ads .

One is Text based Ads and another one is Image Based Ads .

d) Display Ads :

Basically , the display ads appear above the Video suggestions list . These display ads can be managed by making use of google's Adwords .

e) Sponsored Cards & Cards :

The cards or Sponsored Cards are nothing but the pop – ups that have the option of **" Call – to – action "** that we will get at the corner of the video . By making use of those cards you can make the viewer to go to your another video or else to your website or blog .

These cards are really effective because they won't bother the person that is watching the video because these cards don't mess with Viewers playtime , they only expand to their full size when they are clicked .

f) Bumper Ads :

The Next time you come across any youtube Ad that lasts for 5 to 6 seconds which is non – skippable keep in mind that those are nothing but bumper Ads .

<u>9 * GETTING MUSIC FOR YOUR VIDEO</u>

Getting music for your video is very crucial because that's what decides the audience engagement towards your video . **The better the music or the audio that is in the video – the better experience the audience will get by watching that specific video making it popular** . So If you want good music then you can go for youtube's free music or else you can opt for other websites that give you music rights for money .

Its up to you to decide whether you want to include any music in the video or not . If your channel is related to unboxing then you don't have to ad music you can record the video of you describing about the object

(Whether it is phone or laptop or any other accessories) . Then the only thing that you should focus on , is the audio clarity . You can get good audio by making use of high standard microphones or else by making use of your ear phones as well .

<u>10 * SCRIPT AHEAD</u>

You have to plan out your script , do a complete read , re – write if needed . In this manner you will be able to get comfortable while you are trying to convey the content infront of a camera .

You might think that you can directly start shooting without any practice .

But that is not the way . That's not how it works . Keep in mind one thing all the time that " Practice makes Man Perfect " .

Mastering this art of writing script can make you look better in the videos that you make there by taking your videos entirely to a next level .

That's how every successful youtuber made it look so easy on the screen .

Not because they are perfect and Not because they have very high intellect or talent .

It just because of this simple reason that they write the entire script over and over to look for modifications there by getting perfection in every content .

<u>11 * MAKE FIRST FEW SECONDS MOST ATTRACTIVE</u>

Did you know that 20 to 25 percent of the viewers watching the video drop off with in first 10 to 15 seconds . This is the reason why you need to make the most out of the first few seconds in your video .

 But at the same time the video should be catchy to eyes . So Don't see this as a task , instead use this window of opportunity and tell what you are trying to show to the viewer so that you will grab the viewer's attention .

Even If you pay attention to the ads that you see in television , that's how they too do it . . .

By Making the first few seconds of the video attractive the value of the video will be changed to next level .

<u>**12 * ADDING CTA IN TO VIDEOS**</u>

Every youtuber knows how to create **" call – to – action "** or CTA . But Doesn't know how to create it in a powerful way so that users will get a link to another video in the same channel or else user might find link to another channel if he or she clicks the call to action button .

Youtube has mafe this easy by allowing content creators to add End screens and cards in to their videos .

End Screens :

Yes , You heard it right ! An End Screen is just what it sounds like . It is nothing but a portion of screen where a call to action will appear at the end of your video . If you want to Encourage Viewers to promote your website you can do with the help of these End Screens . You can have multiple Links per End Screen .

Cards :

If you Find It Difficult to promote anything by means of End – Screens you can go for cards . These cards allow you to add more interaction on your video screen . It helps pointing viewers to a specific link or showing a playlist or even promoting a channel .

<u>**13 * KEEP TITLES & INTRO SHORT**</u>

Attention spans are too short for any viewer . So a long title or credit sequence at starting of the video can make people lose interest on the entire video that you have uploaded . So it is better to make your opening title and credits short . If it's possible for you , try to put title using good keywords and the Credits displayed in the video has to be less and as well as intro has to be completed in less than 5 to 6 seconds in that way it would be comfortable for the viewers to watch the video and get to know about your channel in very less amount of time with in that specific time period .

As mentioned before , keep in note that the titles that you Use will make a lot of difference . one such example is my video . . .

<u>**THE ABOVE VIDEO GOT VIRAL WITH IN FEW TIME**</u>

14 * CREATE CUSTOM THUMBNAILS

Video Thumbnail is nothing but the cover of your youtube video that you have uploaded . So you have to make it look good and Engaging . you Don't have to feel surprised if I say that the video thumbnail is the most important thing that decides whether or not a visitor is going to play the video . You can also Add your Photo in the thumbnail making the video look more interactive . So there are lot of ways to create thumbnails using tools available for your PC .

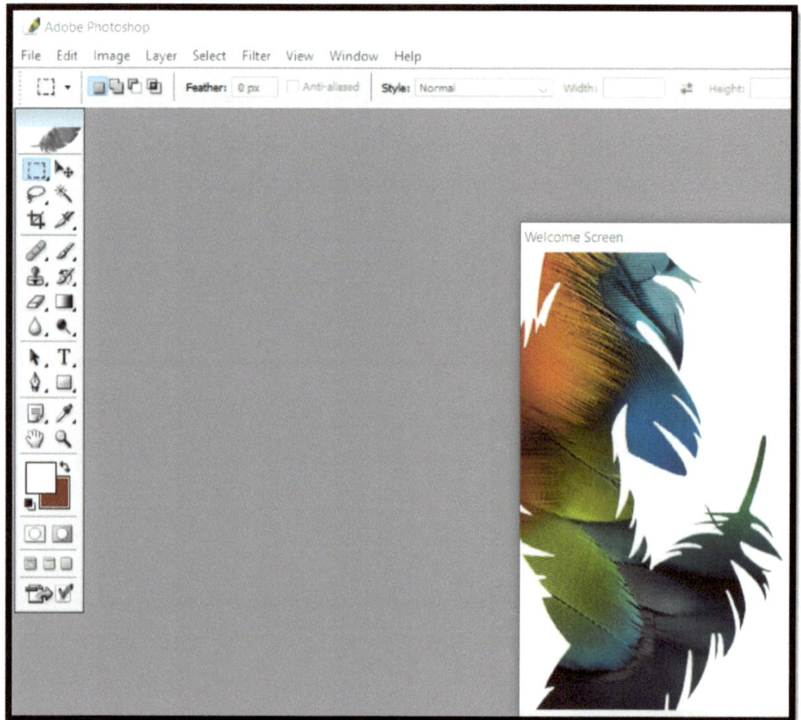

One way is to take a screen shot from video that you have uploaded and add text and Images in that screenshot by making use of photoshop . As shown in the previous page .

Another way is to let the youtube select the thumbnail for you automatically . . .

Above shown is the thumbnail of one of my video - As you can see It is not the best way to let youtube select the thumbnail – Because we can't describe what is in the video in some times with the thumbnails that are automatically generated by youtube .

The other way is to make use of tools available in online . One such tool is tubebuddy .

<<< If you Don't know what is Tube Buddy and how it works .

Don't worry I have clearly explained about it in 17th chapter >>>

15 * OPTIMIZE YOUR YOUTUBE VIDEOS

Every Youtuber should know how to optimize their videos so that their channel can survive in today's youtube world .

You often see that the Youtube Videos are optimized to get good rank in the search Engine Results right . . . !

For this , you need to get familiar with the word SEO which is nothing but **Search Engine Optimization** .

If Needed you can also do specialization in SEO Course so that you can add Tags and Keywords on your Own .

Because it is important to figure out what kind of titles and what kind of keywords the Search Engine is focusing on .

 If you know how to put catchy keywords and if you know what are the trending tags available out there in online then your content will get more number of clicks and views and there by you will get more traffic to your youtube channel and in turn the revenue that is generated by means of your videos will be high . . .

 In turn you will get more money ,

 That's how optimising your youtube video makes a difference in monetization .

The displayed screen shot shows you how I have used keywords in the title . . .

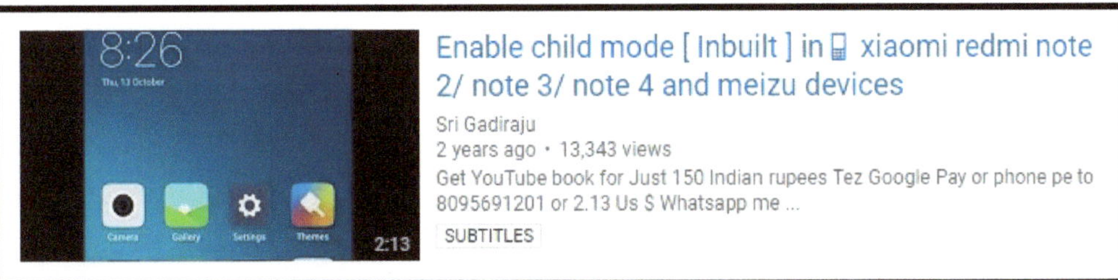

I have used keywords like "redmi" , "note" , "devices" in the Title , which were most searched keywords at that time . . .

Likewise you should adapt to Now-a-days terms and keywords . . .

For you to increase your SEO capabilities . . .

and there by increasing views which in turn will generate lot of money to you by means of monetization .

<<< If you Don't know what is monetization and how it works .

Don't worry I have clearly explained about it in 18th chapter >>>

<u>16 * CREATING VIDEO CAMPAIGN BY MAKING USE OF AD WORDS</u>

These are the steps that you need to follow for creating a video campaign (For Creating AD)

1) Click on **campaigns** on main Toolbar Section

2) Click **+campaign Button** and then select **New Campaign**

3) Select **Video** as your campaigning type

4) Select your **campaign goal** and **subtype** in the options available

5) **Name** it .

6) **Enter the Budget** that you have decided .

7) **Enter Locations** where you want your video to appear

8) **Enter target audience** for the Ad .

9) **Name your Ad** Group in the available selection

   Go for Bid Amounts selection and then select people to target

10)   **Select** video and **your Ad Format**

11)   **Save it** and that's it you are good to go ...

There are some things that you need to take care of for the Ad to get it posted :

The Video should be in any of these formats : MPEG-4 , MPEG-2 or H.264 . The Audio should be in AAC format or else MP3 Format . The

Video's Frame rate should be near to 30 Frames Per Second and the video size should not exceed more than 1 GB . When coming to the resolution of the Ad . It can be 640 X 360 which is 19:9 Ratio or It can be 480 X 360 that is 4:3 ratio .

" Tube Buddy " is nothing but a tool that helps you manage your youtube channel .

Tube Buddy helps the content creator Easily grow and manage his youtube account by making use of an option called Bulk Processing you can even Bulk Edit the videos .

YOU CAN

It is launched in the year 2014 and it has been getting updates since then . Now a days lot of famous youtubers use this tool for managing their youtube channels . This tool is available for mobile as well .

Back in the days – I use to do a lot of hard work for the post processing steps that has to be taken to ensure that my video reaches out high Number of Audience . But , guess what it used to take lot of time and energy and that too with all the effort that I put – the videos used to reach very less amount of views . I always use to search for the tool that will help with my work flow and in doing so I stumbled Up on this really cool tool .

I came across this really cool tool for youtubers called **" Tube Buddy "** .

It is the most amazing tool that integrates with youtube . what separates this tool from lot of other tools available in the online market out there is that this tool is a browser plug – in tool .

You can get this tool for your browser by Entering **tubebuddy.com** in the URL tab . . . Like this . . .

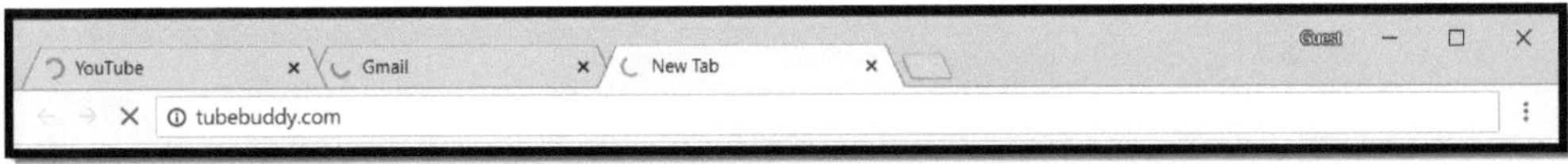

so instead of having to go to separate softwares .

This tool will be integrated with your daily work flow and this tool is great for both beginner and intermediate as well as advanced youtubers .

Have a Look at the **Tool's web page** :

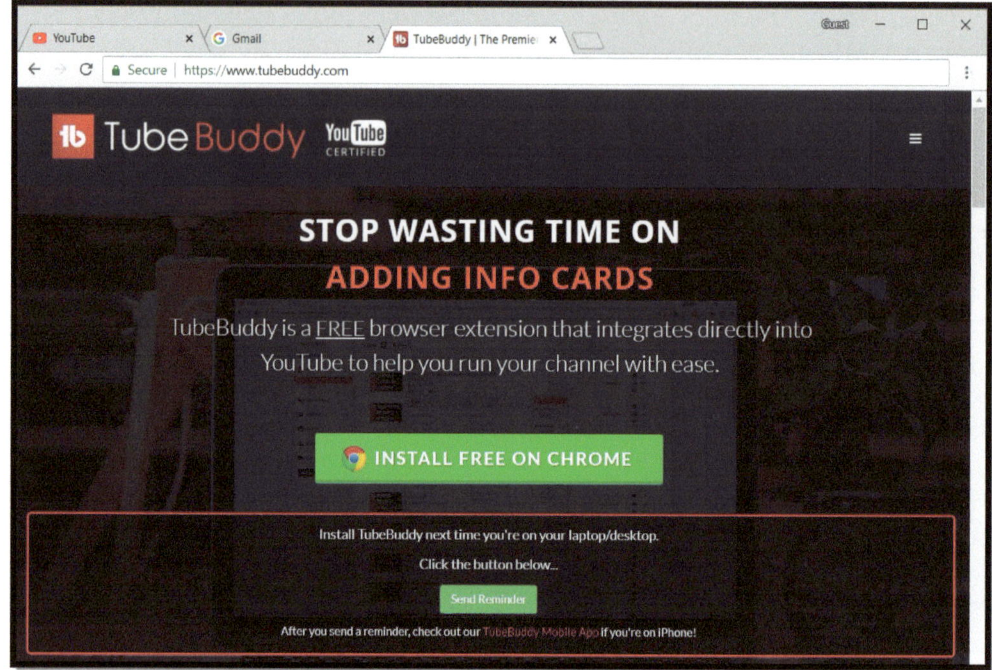

At the beginning this tubebuddy tool used to be for the entry level youtuber . But later on , as the tool got popular , developers added additional features to support advanced youtubers too .

I have used probably every tool created for youtube . But this tool is my key to go now ...

As You know I have been addressing in the book that you need to have better thumbnails and keywords – well this tool focuses on both of them .

The developers of this tool introduced a great feature in to this tool to create amazing thumbnails .

Previously I use to take screenshot of the video and edit it on the photoshop and add Text overlays and resize everything and upload it then ...

But by making use of tube buddy Now I can take still frame from that video and add that along with text and Image overlay right on top of the still image and just by clicking a button we can also save that as a template . I really love this tool .

Even though I know photoshop I found this tool more comfortable and easy . Because once you do this you will find out how easy it is .

Your view count go up automatically .

Now there is another thing that I really like about youtube is that it is integrated with this tool which gives youtube content creators the flexibility to add tags by using " Tag Explorer " available In this tool .

This tool suggests you texts , shows you what trending . But Keep in mind one thing – Don't rely on automated features in the tool Completely .

After all its not in the tool – Its in the person who uses it Efficiently and effectively .

18 * MONETIZATION

Sign in to **youtube** .

In Top Right corner , select your account Icon and then Creator Studio .

In Left Menu , Select channel and then **status and Features** .

Under the Monetization option Click on **" Enable "** .

Follow the on – screen Steps to accept the youtube partner program Terms .

Create **Adsense Account**

If you don't have any ,

As you need the account to **Earn money** .

In order to receive the payments you need to log into your adsense accounts otherwise you won't get any payments .

After creating the adsense account and you have reached your payment threshold then only you will paid for your earnings that you have got because of the ads that had played on your youtube videos

Take care of your videos : If any Copy Right Violation happens then your monetization will be suspended .

Setting monetization Preferences :

Choose what type of Ads you want to run on your videos .

Then select automatically turn on monetization so that whenever you upload any video in future , automatically the video will be selected for monetization .

Also make existing videos Enabled for Monetization .

When you set this , once you start getting Ads on your Videos you will start earning Money .

The last step for monetization is " getting Reviewed " .

Once your channel Meets Certain threshold level the youtube will let you know by contacting you through your gmail associated to your youtube channel .

Once your channel reaches 4000 watch hours your channel will be automatically get eligible for the necessary steps that can we do further to " **start earning money** " .

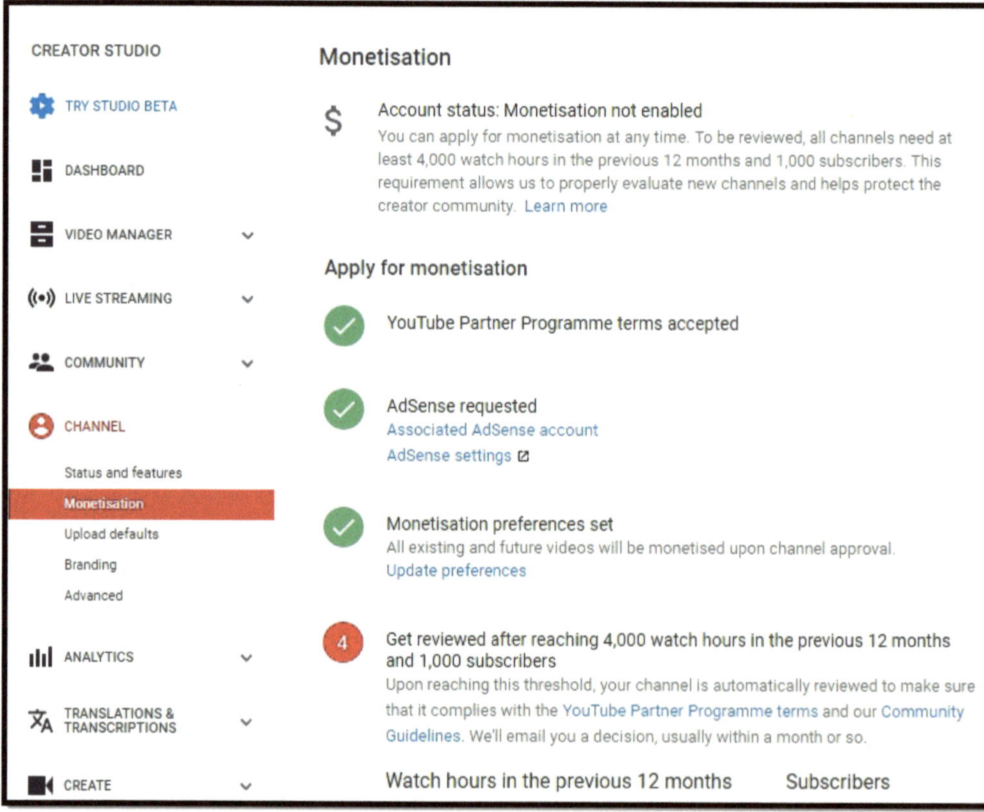

You can Enable or Disable your monetization option by going in to settings :

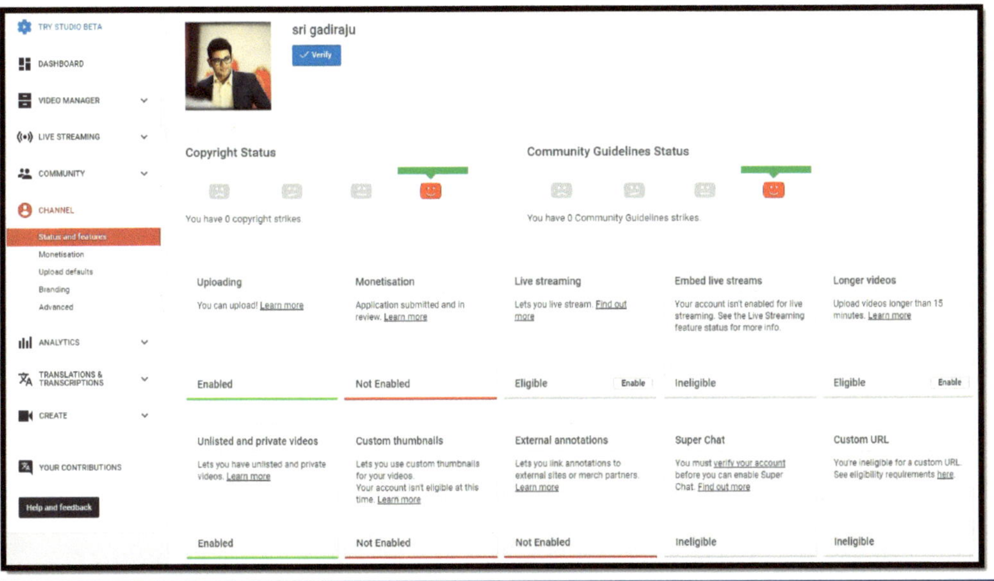

19 * STEPS TO INCREASE TRAFFIC TO YOUR YOUTUBE CHANNEL

There are some steps to be followed for you to get traffic to your channel . They are :

I) As Mentioned before , you have to Choose your thumbnail carefully .

II) Be careful about the keywords that you choose in your video description .

III) Choose your Title Wisely

IV) Add Tags

V) Reply to the comments

VI) Using your photo

I)   Choose Your  **Video Thumbnail**

As you know that I have mentioned previously in this book that Your Thumbnail is what it takes to attract people . Be cautious about the thumbnail that you are uploading . spend some time for it and make it look good . Even though people often say "don't judge a book by its cover" It does not relate in this case to the video thumbnail because it is all needed for the click to happen .

II)   Be careful about the keywords
**   that you choose in your video description**

The Keywords that you use in your description plays a crucial role . There are lot of keyword selection tools available in online now – a – days . Try to use any one of the keyword tool available out there . As Keyword Tool is an extremely useful for youtube Tag generation too , it helps you get more number of viewers .

III)   Choose your Title Wisely

The Title that you choose to give to your video will also play an important role in getting the clicks . Lot of youtubers do the mistake of making the title confusing by using complex words & hence the viewers will not go for the video and in turn leading to less number of clicks .

IV)   Add Tags

The Tags that you use are very important for the video to stand out in the catergories that you wish to focus .

Tags are nothing but descriptive form of special keywords that you can add to your video to help people find your content .

V)   Reply to the Comments

Replying to the comments that you get to your videos will make a lot of difference in getting the traffic to your channel . you should cultivate the habit of replying to as many comments as possible .

VI)   Using your Photo

As you know that people relate to people . But do you know why , there is lot of science behind this . This happens because of the viewer getting used to a person's identity . So let me make this clear , the thing that people relate to . . . is your Face . Yes , you Heard it right . . . ! When you use your Photo in the video's thumbnail Firstly it will drag the attention of the viewer and also try to put your photo in some parts of your video so that the viewer will be interested in your story or information that you are trying to convey .

If you put your photo in your video's thumbnail and in other parts of the video . The Viewers will relate to you .

<u>20 * GEAR TO RECORD VIDEOS</u>

As lot of famous youtubers upload a high quality content you might be thinking that they became famous because of using good Gear . But that's not true

you don't need to have a high quality DSLR camera to record videos – you can do that with the help of your smartphone

The same with microphone – you don't need to buy a costly mic set to record audio you can do that with the help of you ear phones . Try it once – You will be surprised by the results .

" Well This should not have to be the same for every person "

If you can afford a little bit then you can go for a DSLR and stuff like that

If you want to go for Cheap Camera's then you can opt for Canon 1300 D , 1500 D that costs somewhere around 27,000 depending up on the

lens available and If you want the camera to cost less than that then you can go for canon 3000 D that costs somewhere around 22,000 with the normal 18-55 mm kit lens or else you can go for Nikon D3500 which comes as an entry level DSLR .

If you have shaky hands then I suggest you to go for a Tripod .

Now – a – days Tripods are available in the online markets (Flipkart and Amazon) From Rs . 500 /-

Please be advised that I am not promoting any brand .

If you are recording from your mobile phone and you want to add some **Cinematic Effects** to the video that you are shooting then you can make use of the device called **Gimbal** .

Lot of Companies manufacture this . By making use of this you will get 360 Degrees pan access and tilt access for your mobile .

 what I mean by that is you will be able to rotate your phone very smoothly focusing on to a specific subject . you can also go for sliders if you want cinematic shots – there are lot of gliders available in the market from low range to mid range and the high range gliders are used by professional photographers .

In the End ,

It is up to you to decide whether to go for quality gear relying on accessories or to have faith in your talent and produce quality content Just by using the things available to you .

21 * CAN A PERSON CHOOSE YOUTUBE

AS A FULL TIME JOB 

It all depends on the educational qualification that the person has ...

The reason I have Pointed out this statement is that , If a person is in his early teens and getting into college – he should be focusing on his studies .

At the same time if that person has passion for youtube content creation , then he can give some time for it . But the priority has to be given to his education first .

Let's consider another scenario , where a person did not pursue any degree and don't have any education background and he is making a living on mobile shop – in this case he can rely on youtube by recording mobile unboxing and reviews .

So its all up to the person ... Do what you **Love** and see the seed called your hardwork blossom to a beautiful Flower .

?

<u>**Let me ask you a question** . . .</u>

Is it Ok to rely on someone in an examination hall for you to pass that particular exam .!

 Hahaha ... !

Well you know the answer . Right ... !

The chances are 50-50 . Likewise Don't blindly follow some youtuber out there who got popular .

*** Make your own mark and stand out ***

You can learn some tips from that youtuber if you want , apart from that its not recommended to copy some other's content and in my perspective I Don't feel Satisfied if the content that I am uploading is not my own .

So I Suggest you to make your own content and make it interesting as well and then upload it .

I am sure that you will be getting subscribers and viewers as well .

But you need to give it time,

Because remember patience is the key to success .

<u>**23 * WHAT IS CONTENT VIOLATION**</u> **?**

First of all , Let us be clear what is meant by Violation . As all of us know Violation is nothing but the Act of violating something or someone . Now here in youtube terminology content violation means Violating the youtube terms and conditions by uploading a Video which does not come in to terms with youtube creator community .

In Most of the cases , video removal happens as a result of **" Copyright Violation "** or nudity content or Excessive violence in the video that you have uploaded or duplicate match to another video that has already been copyrighted .

If any youtube content creator Flags a video in your channel then those flagged videos are reviewed around the clock by youtube staff members for a variety of reasons .

If you flag a video or someone flags your video , it does not necessarily mean it will be taken down as youtube company itself states that the videos in youtube will be removed only if that particular video has violated the youtube guidelines .

If you think that you have not violated any rules by means of your youtube channel but still . . .

if your monetization is disabled temporarily , then you can send feedback to youtube by going in to your channel Icon and then click on send feedback . . .

so that a feedback will be sent to the youtube team .

you can send the feedback –

As shown in the below screenshot :

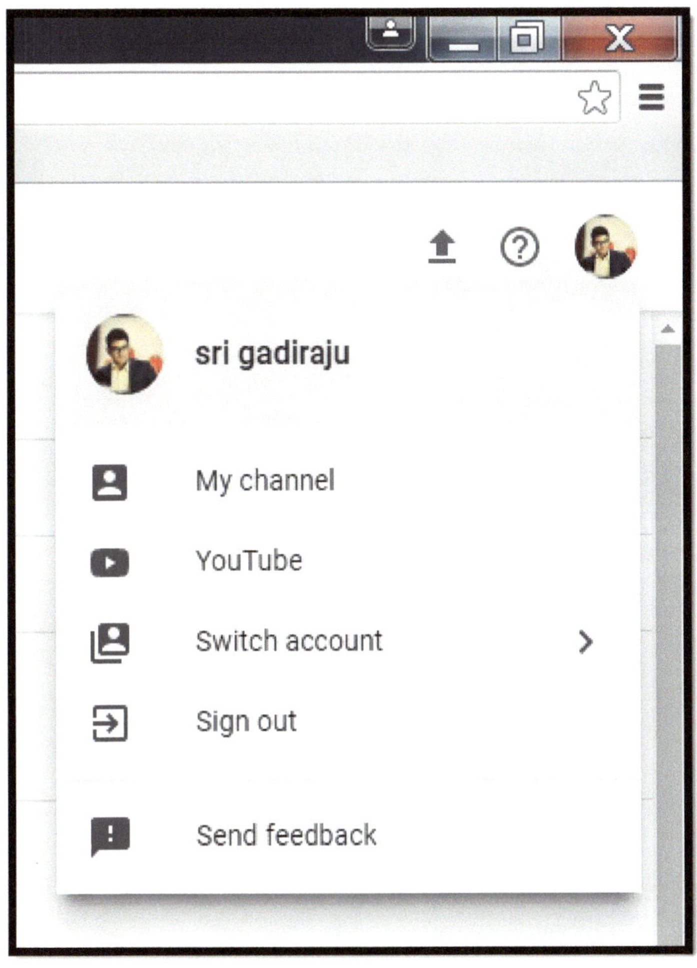

You might wonder how the video that has been blocked will be displayed to others right . . . ?

Well this is how it looks like . . .

24 * WHAT SHOULD WE DO WHEN OUR VIDEOS GOT BLOCKED ?

Sign in to your **Youtube** Account

In Top Right , Click your **Account Icon** As I mentioned before you can do that by . . .

 Clicking **Creator Studio** Setting

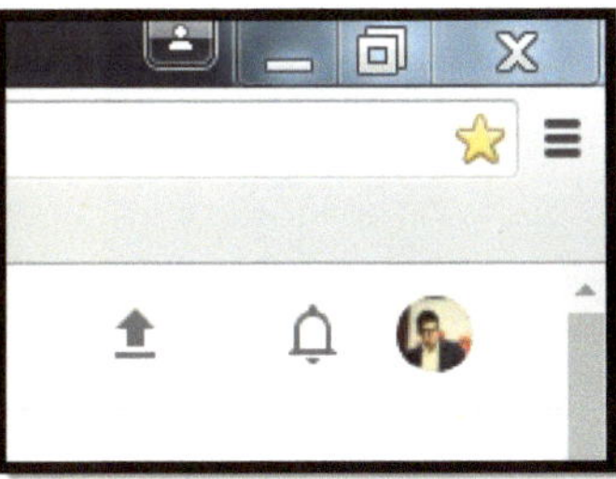

On the Left , Click **Video Manager** Button

Select **Copy Right Notices** Option

Click Copyright Strike Next to a video to Learn more about the Video Removal .

You can also go into creator studio settings by typing https://studio.youtube.com in the URL bar

Most of the times youtube will not remove videos from any one's youtube channel . But if it has been found that your video belongs to some other person . Then youtube will send you a notice to remove it . If you have received these kind of notices more than 3 times then that's it .

Your Adsense account will be blocked .

& you will not get any other chance to claim for your account balance and all the amount that you have earned till that point will be lost and you will lose the option to monetize again . The youtube has several algorithms running in place together to prevent the copyright Infringement , but some times these algorithms and tools often flag perfectly legal videos along with the Bad ones . So if in any case your video has been hit with content ID claim , there are several things that you can do to get the claim removed . If you have copyright strike on any one of your videos then you can file a counter notification stating that your video belongs to you If your video falls under fair use and if you have not used any wrong content .

Understand why you may have received a Content ID claim :

Content ID is nothing but a system that selects potential copyrighted content in videos by scanning uploaded videos with previously uploaded videos in the youtube data base . The youtube algorithm will scan for audio and video and any other data such as images . If by chance any match is there , then the original owner of the video will be notified and there by a content ID claim is filed . Now its up to the original owner to choose any further action . He can do nothing about it and simply stay calm or else he can mute their audio in your video if any or even block the video if it belongs to him

Decide if you want to do anything :

First keep in mind one thing that the Content claims are not always a negative thing for your youtube channel – In the sense some times the claim will be only for audio . Then you can do one thing with the video that you have , you can block the audio with the video being running .

Remove Music or Change it :

Just think if your claim was because of a song being used in your video or because of any music being used then you can try youtube tools to take song or music out of that particular video by going into video manager and then "edit" and simply clicking on "remove this song" .

Enable shared Monetization :

If you are a youtube partner and the video that you have uploaded qualifies certain terms and conditions then you have a chance to share the revenue that is generated because of that video .

In the sense ,

If a gray "$" symbol is appearing next to the video then it means that the content owner has enabled the **Revenue Sharing Feature** On his end . So that the revenue will be shared for both of you .

Opening Copy Right Notices :

You can directly open it directly at youtube.com/my_videos_copyright

25 * CAN WE HAVE TWO YOUTUBE CHANNELS ?

First of all , It's an individuals' choice . I don't want to make any comments on this . But let me explain the science behind this . Having two youtube channels means having two Brandings to get you the revenue by means of it . Essentially having multiple channels of youtube account means that you need to have corresponding google plus page . So the only thing that you have to do is hit the new " Swtich Accounts " in the settings and then click to show all my channels . On that page there will be Create New channel button .

You are also allowed to monetize multiple youtube channels but the thing is you will only get one Adsense account if you are having only one gmail .

Also Remember that the channels have to be approved or invited for the youtube partnership .

So Let's get in to the question " **CAN WE HAVE TWO YOUTUBE CHANNELS** " .

Yes There is No problem with that . . .

First Let us break it Down in to pieces .

→   How does collaboration with other channel works &

→   Is collaboration really Needed ?

Collaborating with other channels gets the traffic from the other channel that you have collaborated in to your channel and there by increasing the number of the viewers and subscribers . In other words , Collaborating with other channels means having a meet together in online and letting both of the youtubers' fans to inform that they are trying to increase their community .

You can collaborate a playlist on youtube by going in to video manager and then into playlists and Next to that there will be an option available to **Collaborate** on . Click on that and check the box that say " Allow people with the link to add videos " . Copy that link for your playlist and share it with the youtubers that you want to Collaborate with .

Coming to the question " whether it is needed or not " , I think it is . . . A yes

As collaborating increases the subscribers , viewers and as well as fan base .

I never found it difficult to share the links of my youtube videos to outsiders . you know why because I have got the **QR codes** with me all the time whenever I travel to other places so that I can share the links to my videos and the links to my blogs right ahead by making use of **QR codes** .

This is how I do it . . . !

I Embed the links to **my youtube videos** in to a **QR code** and I print that QR code in my visiting card and Whenever I meet new people

I give them my visiting card in which all of my information is stored .

Back in the days For my old channel , I use to give my links and the people has to type the entire link for my channel like this :

But Now by making use of QR codes , I have created the window of opportunity to create and embed several links in to one QR code and there by making it easy for the people to go to all of my channels and blogs .

YOUTUBE SIMPLIFIED

If you want to **change channel Name** :

You can go into advanced settings in the creator studio options . . .

Like this . . .

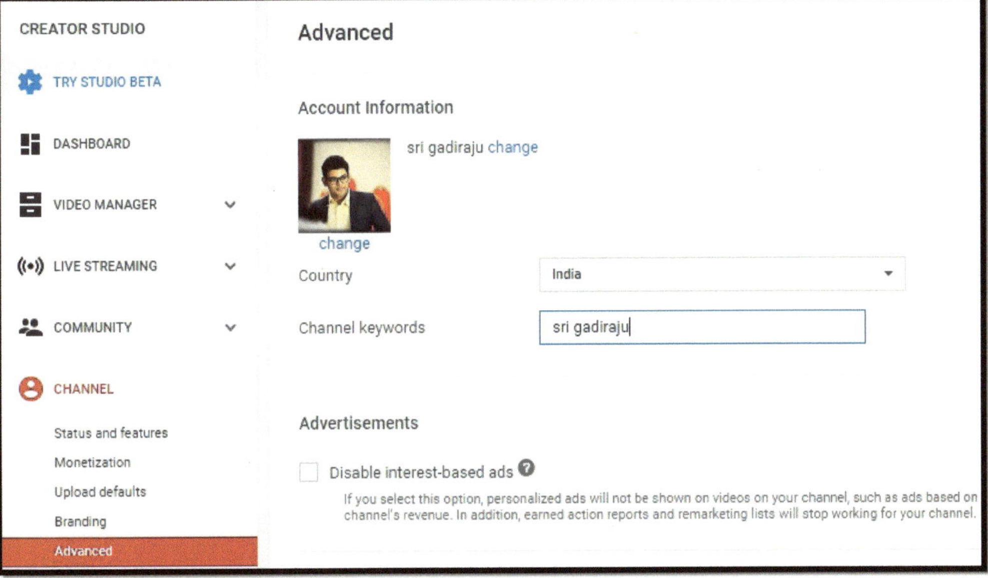

To Add Branding you can go for Branding option and you can add a water mark there . . .

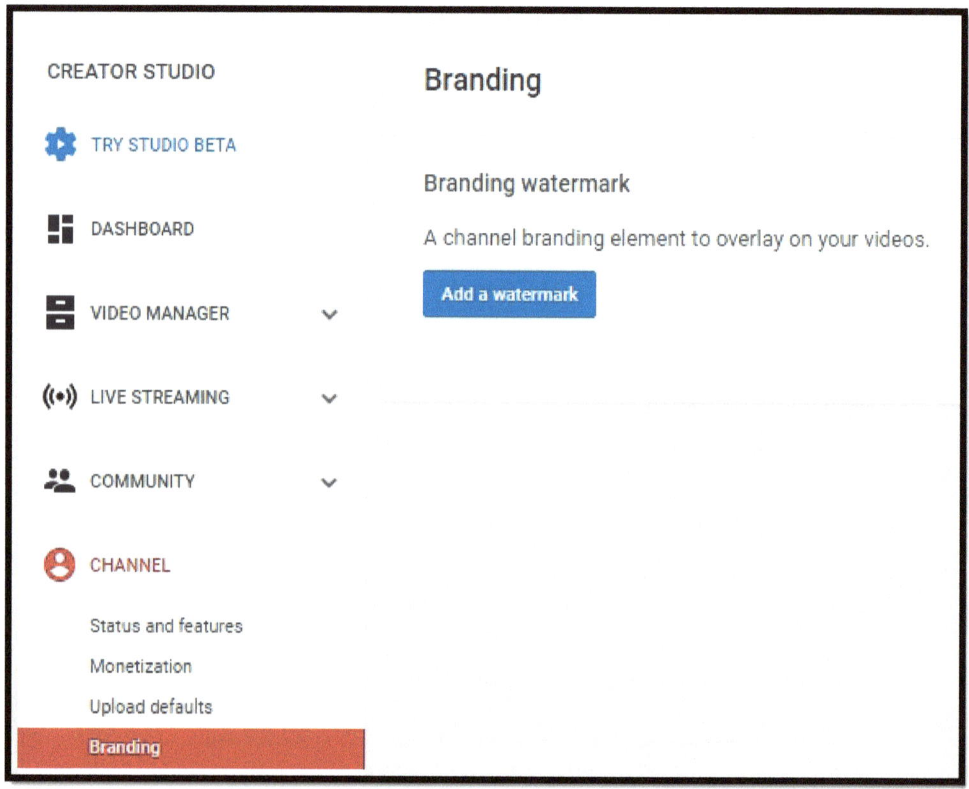

If you want to view any additional settings as mentioned before in the book , click on the settings icon – placed right after creator studio button . . .

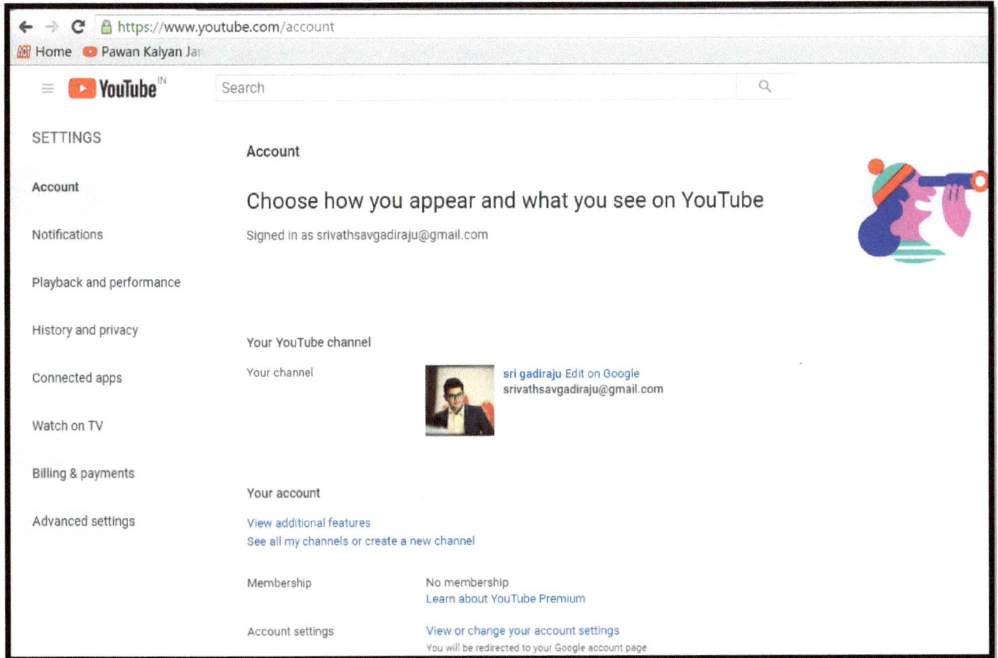

If you want to view the money that is generated by your youtube channel you can see that by going into **channel analytics .**

You can see your estimated revenue as well . . .

I Hope that you have gained some knowledge about youtube from this book

Thank you for Reading

The EnD